Looking for Icarus

Roselle Angwin

Indigo Dreams Publishing

First Edition: Looking for Icarus, Bluechrome, 2005.
Second edition published in Great Britain in 2015 by:
Indigo Dreams Publishing Ltd
24 Forest Houses
Halwill
Beaworthy
EX21 5UU
www.indigodreams.co.uk

ISBN 978-1-909357-88-4

British Library Cataloguing in Publication Data. A CIP record for this book can be obtained from the British Library.

Designed and typeset in Palatino Linotype by Indigo Dreams.
Author photo Francis R Jones
Cover design by Ronnie Goodyer at Indigo Dreams from an image by Gay Anderson.
Printed and bound in Great Britain by 4edge Ltd.
www.4edge.co.uk

Papers used by Indigo Dreams are recyclable products made from wood grown in sustainable forests following the guidance of the Forest Stewardship Council.

Acknowledgements

Some of these poems have appeared, often in earlier versions, in The Rialto, Fire, The Journal, Orbis, Borderlines, Oasis, Stride, 10th Muse, Contemporary Haibun, on Exeter Cathedral website, and in anthologies: Voices For Kosovo, Plymouth Poetry Exchange anthology, Blue Nose competition anthology, Shamanic Warriors Now Poets, In the Presence of Sharks, Into the Further Reaches.

Also by Roselle Angwin

Riding the Dragon – myth and the inner journey; Creative Novel Writing; Avebury; River Suite; A Hawk Into Everywhere and *The Present Where* with Rupert Loydell; *Hestercombe Prints and Poems*, a hand-made artists' book with printmaker Penny Grist, and an Arts Council book, *Writing The Bright Moment – inspiration & guidance for writers; Imago; The Burning Ground; Bardo* and *All the Missing Names of Love*. *River Suite* has appeared as a limited edition artists' book, with photographer Vikky Minette.

CONTENTS

Looking for Icarus

West

Collytown

Cutting a blade of grass and shaking the universe: the implicate order. The whole tree being the forest. One child being all people. One breath breathing all the winds of the universe. Weeks of rain; I'm stumbling down the track, and somewhere – the other side of the world – my footstep sets a tumble of dust trickling. There you are, out there somewhere, and I don't see you, can't touch you, but turning might catch a sudden scent of you on the breeze, the tremor of you flickering through these thistles and dry grasses.

Vellator

Taking all of forever. Stream bank; marsh marigolds; meadowsweet and yellow flags. Red Devon cows' tongues' lazy tugging. White noise of insects.

Still the handprints, not quite swallowed into distance. In my hair.

Once, long ago, there was a country.

How the tides turn inside us.

Night's beaches: a scattering of cowries: galaxies or freckles. Shoreline stretching further than we can see.
A million miles between solar plexus and heart, says Bly;

and longer still the stride from one heart's dark nebula to another.

St Ives

Today, paradise. Synaesthesia: everything is everything else. Sensory overload; no space for emotion. Sea-light. Lichen-roofed houses, Island chapel, soft gold sand, parabolas of mussels. Herring gull stalled in the air above you, yellow eyes scanning. Tall latte in a glass. Garlic bread, hummus, olives, roast aubergines and peppers with goat's cheese. Two seals in the shallows. Sun. Hot. Sun.

...and for a long space of that day you were voyaging in the Sea of Clear Glass, a sea of such purity that the gravel and sand of the sea were clearly visible through it; and you saw no monsters or beasts therein among the crags, but only the pure gravel and the green sand...

St Ives
Night – opalescent. Towards Lyonesse. Godrevy blinks.

The legend's black and white sails. To arrive too late, or never to arrive at all? *We create the habit of forgetfulness*

and back to the dying fall. *This is not what I wanted to say / this is not it at all.* The sea lapping and lapping; something misplaced, forgotten at the margins of your mind. Human voices wake you. All those lost lands.

And then the sea that is thin like mist that seems as if it will not support your boat.

Exmouth
Poems: all tidelines and textures. A moment here which we can catch; this world's elastic and it'll run through our fingers like sand and still not be lost. Summer starts here: this beach, this blue untroubled sea, this single oystercatcher balanced; this breathing. Side-by-side. Talking's a kind of silence. This kind of silence can stop the world: let us climb out of our separate histories into this salt-licked day.

Streaming into, and through, each other.

Bere Ferrers

Caesura: it happens that the spaces in the blackbird's song can break your heart as surely as splinters of glass. It happens that what is not said costs more than what is. It happens that it hurts. It happens. Above, something's flying too high up. It happens that you can barely see. It happens that a morning arrives when you wake and look out, and a bright spring is running away between whispering grasses; running away, drying up.

Hartland Quay

Welcombe is horizontals, grasses, the sound of the stream, dog barking in the shallows where your skirt hem is laced with salt. A cave. The ghost of fires we lit twenty years ago... Speke's Mill Mouth gives us sudden hail, a waterfall, rainbow, solitude, dinosaur-egg-rocks. I'd forgotten the water gardens: gunnera, Earl Grey, other people's conversations, two vintage bikes leaning together, soft green darkness. The valley closing over us, a *now* before the future wraps us. Then Hartland, not what I want today: rasping verticals, treacherous crevices, world sliced away. Too much of leaving in every direction.

Bere Ferrers

Questions of fire, earth, air, water. Questions of courage, of risk and safety. Questions of what must remain unspoken and what trouble the unsaid might cause. Questions of gaps and pauses and silence. Questions of music and dancing and song. Come closer, go away. On this June morning the landscape blazes with barley and birdsong. On this June morning the river's broad body's an invitation, an injunction. You're holding hands. One of you jumps, the other does not. Who is it who keeps falling, falling in the bright air?

Saunton

Vernal equinox. Equal day and night. The gales have loosed pebbles all over the beach. The far cliffs are lagged with the sharp green of mesembryanthemum, though it's belting down and I can barely see them. I've given up trying to be cool and impress you: straggles of bedraggled hair whip my face and I'm sure I've smudged mascara. We're walking on the swallowed village – wind in the right direction you can still hear the bells.

No division between
dirty-grey sky
dirty-grey sea
dirty-grey sand

but between shore and skyline are furious ragged breakers.

The dog yaps frantically and is swallowing a lot of sand. Perhaps you hate dogs?

None of this matters.

First spring rain; in the lanes the fat tide of green, returning.

Lundy

Tasting a moment: stillness at the heart of all matter. We are newcomers to reality: still just becoming. *Only connect.* The boat bumps the jetty and triggers a trickle of stones. Seal, razorbill: mere thickening of the atoms which make up water. Light glances off everything: it dissolves into everything and everything dissolves.

It is possible that you drown...

South Hooe

Dawn. Your greenness is sharp on my tongue: lime juice, lemongrass, sap. Ozone is the shape you make in my nostrils;

you're salt on my lips. Your easterlies comb the clouds into the long humerus of angels. My backbone prickles with your knowing. You nail constellations onto bare black branches; one after one flaring; dominoing into white flame.

Mothercombe
Cliff-path's thick with summer – ragged robin, woodruff, vetch. Tight sharp blackberries, pink-fleshed. Stream's shedding song, unthinking. Poised between day and night here where tide floods the creek and sunslicked sea rolls like a cat at our feet. Up to our eyes in it. If you ran a finger round the horizon's lapis rim it would spill arpeggios into your bloodstream.

Collytown
Hungering for silence you want to break free of these distances. The dawn wind's lilac: you want to be here quiet by the window (fragrance, light) or you want to be there with the thunder on the horizon, in yesterday, or tomorrow, searching, searching.

Hungry for distances, you want to break free of this silence.

Dozmary Pool
In the day's darkness here on Bodmin Moor between life and death sits Jan Tregeagle: the Cornish Sisyphus, going down instead of up. Portioning out his life in bucketfuls; and no matter how much he empties, he knows there'll always be more...

Sancreed Holy Well
The steps down, the source
these are the new oases
sacred delphic wells

voices from the time when gods
and goddesses still mattered

see how the copper rods duck and flicker

Nothing but silence
mossed stones, the eye of water
lighting green gloaming

this candled ribboned threshold
this mouth – first light, last darkness.

Wistman's Wood

The wood is all about fusion, but the day is all gaps and edges.
Thinking about death, though as usual I'd rather not. 'Death is
a process,' you say, 'not an event. Concluded by an arbitrary
moment when all attempts at resuscitation seem finally to fail.'
Which makes me think that life must be quite a rare
phenomenon, caught kneeling in random acts of propitiation in
the cracks between failures...

Two Bridges

... later, in the garden, I'm thinking about journeys. Lindsay
Clarke said the Grail Quest was a process, not an event; and I'm
about to tell you, but already you're on the next stepping stone
and declaiming Wendy Cope: the title poem from *Making Cocoa
for Kingsley Amis*. The sun splices the water.

Another moment fallen through the gap.

Hallowell Wood

Who is it who vanishes into the bigger darkness, over the
banks, the water, the gorse-clad wooded hillside with its
arteries of leaching streams? Who fingers stone, bone, moss;
who noses towards air, the rush of wind? Who is it set ticking

by some rhythm in the blood, tidal wave, drift that will not be stilled, who insists on the narrow twisting path towards the thinning light?

Weir Quay
Even the mist, the rain, can blast you out of yourself, cast you dry on the flanks of these mudflats where you stand, feel the blazing pulse of it all still bang through the dock, the fireweed, soles of your feet.

Tamar
Hill's velvet pelt of faraway barley;
at the cusp of the tide the trees' green
smoke. Beyond, the manor house, hidden, secret.
Remember the lily pond, the tunnelling shrubs,
our sudden emergence into that
exuberance of light?

Trebarwith Strand
She's insistent, the ocean, keeps on coming even when you're full of her already. DON'T WANT DROWNING. But there are times when all you can do is let go, stretch out – here on this rock between sea and sky – give over, allow yourself to be taken.

Bere Ferrers
Lily pollen, staining the white windowsill and my hands the colour of sunshine. Walking round the hayfield this morning; air smelling of autumn. Few swallows; blackberries too soggy and too sweet.

The questions we need to ask and the ones we don't.
J's face last night talking of his dead wife's face.

Day rolls in the stubble. Traces of fox and pheasant in the margins. Deer spoor. The wild geese this morning are silent. St John's Wort – the wild one – lifts starry yellow faces.

Wembury

Morning's tide recedes. Bird tracks and strewn black wrack jostle driftwood and limpets. I think of you here; your last day, years away from the wild Hebridean shoreline, its lacing of yellow periwinkles like small fierce suns. *Remember those days,* I say to you. *Remember.* But still I can't stop your falling, over and over, falling.

Some days I walk for hours.

Bere Ferrers

Some days we're made small by the thought that at the heart of it all we shall tumble into nothing. With winter approaching the land's already saturated. The earth can't bear any more cargo. Even corpses, they say, are floating away. These months I'm obsessed by dying, with erosion and absence and departure. Philip Gross: 'everything / bleeds... these last days, bleeds away'; and past the house swirls topsoil, branches, still small sodden animals, bumping up against the stonework, nudging the door. On the phone, I hear you shiver.

Only the dead, I think, aren't frightened of leaving.

South Tawton

Over Cawsand Beacon rises the moon. You hate Cawsand and tonight you hate the moon. You get up and you dance. You pretend not to notice that there's blood on your new white shoes. You grit your teeth. Oh yes it will be all right. It's a matter of belief. You get up and dance. You pretend. There's blood. You grit. All this an absence – something sliding away, hiding, a small damp thing in a small dark corner. You hide, but still you get up and you dance. Enough! cry the feet. Enough! cry the shoes. Enough! cry the locked white teeth. The red tide grows.

Bere Ferrers
This is not a love poem. This is bryony:
bold dark leaves, heart-shaped;
small brief flowers, hidden;
shiny berries, poisonous.

The zigzag path
Places I've never been: the eye in the door. The doorway in the eye through which the spirits of living and dead fly in and out. *Et in Arcadia ego.* Not so much leaving as dreaming. Being dreamt. Into the shadows: how the Judas in me betrayed you. How you forgave my trespass.

Boscastle
The wisdom of flotsam. An ache like fog. You navigate by sound, listening for drowned things. This lover, that place, those words peel away like a bow-wave behind you. Only the present counts. No angels; but listen, the ocean's singing.

Downend
There is a woman here, early. She's collecting cowrie shells: one for each year. It's her birthday. She holds out her hands, cupped. Maybe eighty?

Collytown
The lethargy of winter. Hard frost tightens the furrows. Against the still landscape a harlequin of pheasants, the 'sharp hot stink

of fox'.

You are so close now I can feel your breath in the hairs on my arm. So close.

Rocky Valley maze
Life opens its hands, scatters confetti. Relearning the steps to the centre.

Elsewhere
In another place which we've not visited there's a coffee cup and saucer in sunflower yellow. The cup is upturned and our separate moments have temporarily fused. The tides of us flow together. We walk barefoot through the lemon grove, lick honey from each other's fingers, celebrate the sunshine, the moment. All there is.

Sennen Cove

Blackbird
This is not the colourless season
of margins and absences
This is the black and white time
Sharp in the dawn this one pure note.

Thorn Tree
Wind, monoliths, salt on my lips
This high hinterland furrowed
by plough, waves of lapwing and fieldfare
Me, resilient, gale-swept.

Glass
January's first day, and everything
yet to be broken
Washed, untrodden sand; deep sky;
this wave, caught at its curl's apex.

String
Kelp, green weed, boulders like seals
Everything always the same, and forever changing

I am the tether
of this moment's kite.

Tide
There is the white sand
and there my welling footsteps
There is the prowling tide

and then only water.

On The Beach

ocean
the sea speaks green here
and mauve and mussel-blue

her arms, her foam-flecked lips

her words are rock, are flick
of fish, sway of wrack, whale-song –
one long syllable, vast as night

shore
I have come back to the language
of stone and sand; my voice
laid out like the ribbon horizon
drinking the sky.
                          The footprints
are mine; the words unimportant.

                          It is time.
The stones climb the hill;
winter peppers the shore.

Wait for moonrise; first star
and a single curlew piping the night.

sky
the night of falling stars

one perfect round quartz pebble
a syllable, a god's eye
clear as early love –

we bring it home, a memory –
all night on the windowsill
it sings its pure white note

and outside all the sky, listening

Zennor

And so, after so long, what was it
calling, that pulled me west
to this glass-blue day
at the edge of the land?

And you're there, the flame
of you, amber against the sky's
wide window, against heathered
granite headlands, and a moment

constellates, floods the yards between us,
gathers to itself the day's light
fists into the force
that will uncoil us into a great shout

and fling us, whether we will it
or not, across
this wide, dark river
from which there's no return.

From the Rainblack Ash

In the water gardens the day in their hands
is all scintilla and snakes of water
those coiling ribbons of light –
she needs to lap at it like a dog

down on hands & knees
on the slippy oak walkway
then the enmeshing nets of rain in the cherry
in winter sun; the green day

silhouetting them. It's too much
naming this November 'spring'
but they do, and do
again: that green water on her tongue

the light reframing itself
over & over till her head
is awash with a *Glassworks* pattern
in a minor key, brimming

before the crossroads
& on the blind bend
the pub – the fire, the soup –
(what might have been)

and the urgent words skeining between them
which is not much of a reason
for the hot press
of their side-by-side bodies, though

their brief private joy is; and the vastness of the world
and winter, and the long lonely night –

and that this day will never
be theirs again –

and the crashing horde just outside the doors
of a war they did not choose, and sudden loss
and deaths that are not theirs, but are;

but still, listen, outside now
that one last thrush unspooling song
from the rainblack ash.

Cusp

The wave's apex; that moment when it is poised
like a horse for the leap, and the sea's
haunches under it; when it is clean
as glass, unbroken; a silence sculpted from the surf's noise –

that moment; or another – that gone-in-a-flash
cusp between the you of here, now
putting the kettle on, or maybe that slow
piano passage; and then without really knowing it catching

an unguarded question in his eyes, and the both of you gone
tumbling over the lip, a cascade
from which emergence is not possible until too late
if at all; and the myth of return

merely a shadow between two cast-off lives;
beat, heartstop, between systole and diastole glimpsed

and recognised.

Shaman

A muscled instant, a question
hanging poised for the kill,
and a green storm waiting to break borders,
burst the chest, a frantic flood.

We turn on this moment mind to mind,
wordless now, the language of thigh
to thigh, slipping skins like borrowed truths,
and our rawness is where we meet.

Nothing but cliff between us, cliff
and chill blue air;
and the instant spins, falls in on itself;
and you

      now a wave in my hand
      now a fox
      a burning bush
      then again the hawk's high arc;

and then all the wide sky calling,
the day brilliant with feathers,
answers opening over us
like wings.

Whales

The last night I sit outside
till day has bled itself west over the islands;
Coll with its crescent beaches a smudge
under the horned moon, my hand
cramped on my cooling mug,
and the sea annealed silver;
and they don't come.

                    Still
I leave the window open. Bunched shadows
of deer veer past
wary, a hare nudges
the berry-blue mass of sky.

All night I ebb and flow; I am
the rise and fall of the sea's breathing.

                    A god, when it appears
smacks you awake, does not tread lightly.

              Towards daybreak
cresting the waves, I'm slammed
from sleep by a great flank, dark, shining,
ploughing the thinning air

and when I swing my feet to the floor
I'm plunged chasms down in that single
sonic throb, bone-jarring –

        in freefall now, and all the walls dissolving.

Navigation

Riding the back of the Tamar
our keel cutting clean,
waves peeling away to the margins,
narrow channel, silver
among silvered mud,
hoisting the jib, rope snaking
past our feet, creak of breeze,
the deck tilting
between red and green lights,
Navy flotilla, open sea ahead.

Everywhere the world gives voice
unreservedly, over and over:
day crawling up the sky,
the lights of Saltash
multiplied and returned from water,
taste of light rain and saltspray,
that flock of redwings
crooning in the pines
we left behind,
tea in this blue tin mug.

The sun, still rising.
What we need is faith,
a good wind,
a few kind words.

Towards the Equator

You spoke to me once of flying fish
how they arc across the bows
in a shower of brilliance, like red birds

too soon gone; and something left oscillating
above the sails, like a question mark,
a compass disarranged; or a window

into what we half-remember –
the zigzag tracer trail
of something too perfect to be real

and which bruises like exotic fruit
on touching. Afterwards a wanton resonance
clangs through this waterfall of days.

Here in your arms, in this deliquescent moment
memory's red bird arcs again
but already we're vanishing

each spinning through the other's glittering hoop
then gone back into water, until turning
we slip like stones out of sight.

Magdalen

You stare this thing out, taking the sting
of it, knowing what is true.
What gods love makes of us all.

Ah. Not for anything deny
the sweetness at the heart, the way
it came through honey.

*Forgive them, for they know not
what they do.* And you
will hold your own truth.

Be silent. *I have nothing to say.*
It's a story for him and you alone,
and you will not show it

to those who do not care for truths.
You have always lived outside these bounds.
So you do what you've always done:

hold your counsel, keep your tongue.
Stare them out. Feel
the sting of the first stone.

Cracks

Even without tides the waves here
mumble and chew at the shore.

An exercise in dislocation. Broken things:
your fine artworks, smashed, uncared-for.

Later we walked again by the lakes.
There were other fractures –

watching the coots, how a hen pecked
at a chick, pecked as it squealed, pecked

and pecked again, held it underwater.

Fallen

They've clear-felled the woods –
the eerie stretch where I hated to walk alone
and the two great oaks are gone, though their roots
still writhe in the broken earth.

Even at night now light is everywhere.
Nowhere to hide – for It, for mystery, for owls –
even for me. You can have
too much light.

Under the moon the village is silent.
                              Ebb tide.
        Out on the mudflats the curlews' calls
whistle up unimaginable distances.

Let it be enough some mornings

High tide, a wild morning, wild and stormy,
and you take the leaf-deep stony path
above seal-grey waters
                    where the geese are dragged
through the sodden air like ripped-away prayer flags
in a crazy disordered dance, and the waves
slap hard on the mudflats' flanks,

and for once questions like
what use is poetry, if you're starving, or a refugee
squeezed between torture and war, or bleeding alone
in some dark alley
have momentarily flown, though left you unguarded;

but bent low over the creek the damson tree
drops unremarked a cargo of fruit
on the waters –

mornings like this
grey and green with straggled leaves
and the rain storming the opaque sky

let it be enough now to hear this one curlew keen,
to have one last bedraggled swallow skim the thick air
over your head, see the inkcaps' effortless
overnight arrival,
                    to witness one small flower –
samphire, or a late marsh marigold –
struggling through black mud on its journey upwards

against gravity, pointing the way –
let each day be a small triumph, let it be
two fingers to death.

South Hooe

To stand in mud
and know the flow of blue air
parting round your body

to feel for footholds
to feel your feet hold
to feel your feet held

to be mud, part of mud,
part of mud's harvests.

*

To feel the blue air
splitting round your body
to catch the spill of light

with all of your skin; to be
coming in and going out;
to be another reason

for the wind to dance.

*

To be streaked with mud
saltwind, blue air. To be
held, here in the river's

darkness. To take the harsh cry
of the heron; its bristle
on your body. To take its call
in your own lungs.

*

To be the heron. To be
the head of the otter splitting the water
to be the flow of water
transfiguring that head.

*

To know light.
To know the way it falls
the way it breaks.

To not be afraid of dark
or of the mudflats' swollen flanks.
To swim, and not be afraid
of drowning. To strike out

for where the light shivers
breaching the river's deeper
currents. To feel

blue air parting round your
light-rinsed mud-licked head.
To be recognised by light, by mud,
by water.

Leaving

Wind's a westerly, wild, a storm of horses;
and it's come, the berry-red afternoon of leaving,
the far side of summer and all our stories done.

It's this same wind I craved; and that May rain
battering the new bracken of the slopes,
the fleeting light contouring the tors' shoulders.

The air that tastes of greenness. Leaving,
I caught a pint of that cool moorland water,
brought it with me. Northwards, on the train,

as the sandstone stacks flash by and the hills
flatten out and the red Devon earth darkens and fades
and even day dulls as the train rackets inland

away from the saltlight of the coast, my slick
of water shoots its long silver tongue
down my throat, soothes this absurd longing.

A Passing Only

Samhain – October dawn
Six o'clock and the black and silver valley dressed funereal
but ribbons of blue mist over the brook; a few larch tips like
rusty arrowheads

We need the vertical dimension; have found no substitute for
God

Husks, all of us, through which
the winds of heaven pour

To tread here in rimed grass – withered fields, ochre stems,
tattered black thistleheads, umbels outlined in white, still some
nettles, portly oaks squatting like sheep, quick stink of fox in
your nostrils – still alive, then, the mangy old bird-food thief

To be here in and of this land, this morning, this moment
and call it home
knowing that home can never truly be known

but merely reached out to

The warmth of flesh and the warmth of flesh on flesh; still
never naming anywhere home; this mist, this frost, these falling
leaves; still a passing only

the common language of the flesh our common heresy: an
overlay, a disguise sketched on the invisible, unknowable
fleshless and indivisible

October morning
The redwings are back, crooning over berries or skirring in
flocks over the water meadows.
By the wall, dead montbretia heads stream like prayer flags

We see ourselves more clearly
when we're not looking

Calling somewhere home

October dusk
These nights of the quick and the dead. The earth turns away
from the sun. Something of ancient fire flickers within us still;
we flower like candles in grinning pumpkin faces in someone
else's window

Aurora
Now, tonight, under this shifting coloured sky all this falls
away. You are walking, walking, staff of quickbeam, oiled boots
– the long view, the green note that calls you away over these
hills, where you will be

another indigo handprint on the hem
of night.

Doublewaters

You could have been squatting here forever
almost grown into bank, or become another
rippling ring of light on the dark river.
Twigs have roosted in your hair; your hands
river-stone-cold. Breath feathers the last of the day.

Where do we go each time we close behind us
the door of the present moment? Who
steps forward and who is left behind?
Who still squats by the water when you're
long gone into tree, or bird, or sand?

Iona

Sealight so strong in the room I can barely see the other diners, and I need to remember this place, these colours, the strength of the ocean's reflection that floods my head with this whiteness

> as I write it
> already gone –
> this moment

The island in April is wheeling with birds of passage, alighting in one place, on one moment, which is only ever fluid and transient –

> our stories meet
> at table like migrant birds
> blown together   then apart

Breakfast; smell of toast, coffee, bacon. I choose eggs on spinach with hollandaise on home made bread; my plate is decorated with starfruit and melon and kiwi. Just now Ken got up to leave soon after I arrived, and I sit with my cup alone with the light from the sea filling my eyes, watching the gulls alight and then ascend – one, then two, then three, then one again. The one left did not seem to be deeply nostalgic nor full of abandonment. But we leave parts of ourselves wherever we go – you wouldn't think our hearts would be big enough to go on beating

> across the sound
> gannets in freefall
> ocean paratroopers
> if we could love like that!

I guess it must be possible to bring 'passionate equanimity' to everything, even leaving

> outside on the grass
> Maggie makes the slow shapes
> of tai chi

In front of me now the white sand of the blank page. My hand, moving; trying to find a way to imprint on paper the spill of people who have lit my life, the thousands I carry with me and who carry a little of me, too, in their blood –

> we meet
> we are changed
> we move on

The same and not the same. My journey here is my journey everywhere. My journey to you is the same as my journey to me; our lives border the same sea. But this *particular* quality of light, the way it falls in *this* precise moment where I meet you, where our shadows merge, no matter how far each of us travels, will never come again...

> this white sand
> those seabound footprints

> not coming back

Wanting

Rain, freezing. Day breaks like a bruise, pigeon-purple, a suffusion of morning. A flocking day, you say; and all the unborn words that cluster in the corners of rooms gather at the window's candle like moths

the book falls open on midday
a centrefold of laughter and oblivion
rain continues

In the cathedral a dusting of prayer on the stones. Our shadows fan across the nave, touch. Wanting the kind of faith that holds up the roof, stops the sky from falling in, goes leaping and bounding out into the sodden mudstreaked streets, singing.

Cello Suites

i
Rostropovich, King's College Chapel

It was there, between us, palpable –
wrapped in blue air, outlined almost
in gold, like dust from the wings
of an angel (if such things existed),
damming the music in its flood
like a heavenly blood-clot, clenching
ventricles, nailing the heart
to the great ribbed vaulting (this landbound
ark) and one of us crying, it's not
clear who, as if for joy, or loss; and the dust
stirs briefly like the tremors of love
satisfied, or of grief. And it's gone

and you catch yourself thinking
this is the moment; this mystery,
this is where history starts.
And somewhere else a wing unfurls;
here, you're caught up once
and lifted, shipwrecked, drowning.

ii
Steven Isserlis, Exeter Cathedral

After all those words
a river of uncluttered notes.
'I'd like to be voiceless now
for days,' you whisper.

Something beyond language
opens its wings inside us;
bears us out streaming
into blue silence.

Elsewhere

Moments when the street beneath
falls away and you walk upon
holy ground, unmapped, tuned
to another frequency than our own;

or, owl-winged, drift like a scarf
of mist over the dark river,
or kited playful by sneaking gusts;
wherever, you trawl your familiar

flesh over unfamiliar land
and shudder then as you know
yourself unknown. And yet
something ancient – race memory

or instinct, an unseen hand, or tides
of blood and bone that recognise
the star maps, heed the currents,
know the codes – will buoy

you up and track your footsteps,
keep the night's unspeakability
away until you come to green
and find another word for home.

Wild

You have gone too far into the darkness;
there is no other word for it. You have
given up your name, what made you
human. You live now at the crossroads
'entre chien et loup'. We who love you
can no longer reel you in.

What you were circles in its own self-
referring echoes, a distant shout
on the drizzling wind which swam
through these leaves an hour ago
or a lifetime.

In memoriam, then, I shape
these words; touch a finger to
the nouns that you might still inhabit:
tree, rock, river, heron, wolf.

Anima

I see it in your eyes
you've been in exile
thought that England
was a dirty word

here as we wind the last
bends and everything falls
into dusk in a shower
of gold-backed birds

here as we slow
in this ancient courtyard
to the tempo of another time
I see it in your eyes

you think you're in love
with me. But what you
really seek is refuge:
to be seduced at last by
home

Boswednack

Gorse is aflame again; yellow,
the colour of desire,
spitting sparks into the stormy April dusk.

Here at the world's edge,
where sea and sky
devour the stony land,

the night-time air is winged
with voices, and constellations
cram our blood.

Shoreline

Evening's receded to silver and lilac
pewter-banded out past the headland.
The ocean's left smaltings of herself
lolling in rockpools; sand alive
with shrimp fleas. Daytime's trippers
are tided up in shoals washed up
in Devon's hinterlands. We trail
our footprints languorous along the shore.

Let these moments be enough; carry
this gentle walk into night's absences.
Turn away from whisperings beyond the dunes
soft on the westerly breezes; ignore the tug
of routes not taken, words unsaid;
don't heed the ghosts of other lives
stepping where we retreated
keeping our feet dry, hearts almost intact.

Learning the Language

we come from so far away
each of us

seeking the sacred mountains
and the Other

stumbling tongues essaying
the *lingua franca*
behind words

still love to do with becoming
more   not less
oneself

this trying to live wide open
the saying *yes*
the trust

while the head holds tight
and the heart like a
March hare

day after day leaps forward
into darkness

every time
the first

Yew

the falling of light
and the place where it pooled
between us

if you were to come back now
I would eat your red berries

Bristol Airport 5 a.m.

North into night
where the stars stretch out
their tinfoil distances

or – another scenario – wink
in the unlit reaches
of an indigo lounge filled with smokers

you don't want to climb
you're not doing too well
winded with chill and approaching departure

want to duck the constellations
curl into yesterday's softer corners
make yourself small

but there's another way – even
if you miss the morning drive into it
wait for sky to be rinsed of night

making the shapes of dawn –
translucence of lemon, lime –
even if you can't see
turn east, be woken, take off.

Taking to light where staying and going converge

It always seems to be time to move on
we're continuously in transit
even here, in sitting meditation with nowhere to go but the wall

Always looking to leave, restless as winter migrants
and thin with regrets for not staying

Those who have made it in moments
all say the same thing:

look at the flower, look twice
stare into the heart where it burns
let go of your holding, addiction to movement or stasis
fall towards the source, don't look back

Quit with a smile on your face

Hepworth In St Ives

Pull
of the wood's sinew
the tensioned cords singing

I am that figure in the landscape
the greying shadow on the wind

this stone my ancient yearning
my weathered breasts these hills

sound the strings between us all
watch the way we
fall

Box

Tonight I've lost it
at sea in my own blood

dreams awash: Tibet Kosovo Afghanistan
Tiananmen Falklands Iraq

too much. Am drowning.
Fingerprints on walls; an outline

shipwrecked on the flagstones.
Which way home? Rome still burning

Babylon still lost. The fiddle stumbles.
Everywhere a numbing: this wide-blue-eyed

complacency of silence. No-one
remembers how to talk

or what will lay down bridges,
hold us up. Forgetting

how grass grows; what makes
a blackbird, or a spring.

Front Page

They're eloquent, his hands – long,
fine-boned. Beautiful. In their palmed silence
they talk; could almost be at prayer.
I cannot see his face.
I stare; think I have never seen
such hands. Young hands, I'd guess;
but look, a wedding band dulled
by mud. A moment of grace
almost you might think; but
he's grounded, still form shrouded
to the wrists. And then you glimpse
the blood, a glint of handcuffs.

Say

Say there were no guns
say war was illegal.

Say no child was ever tortured
in the long scream of a dark cellar.
Say no-one bled alone in midnight alleys.

Say there was no greed:
no-one was hungry, or homeless.

Say the blind could see
and life-support machines
had taught the almost-dead to dance.

Say we championed dissidents.
Say Biko and Ken Saro-Wiwa
had never had to exist

and Auschwitz wasn't even a figment.
Say there was no death.
Say fear was as foreign as Mars.

Say we could promise to love one another
forever.

Would we have to invent the dark
as a place in which to hide?
Would we need death?

Ashes

The women stand apart. It's the big hats
you notice, tight faces eclipsed.
Mary closed up like a winter lily.

Your name wrong. Twice. Gasps
from the congregation. The matching curtains
and chrysanths, the well-oiled tracks.

Outside we speak in monosyllables
touch and don't quite touch
your name, which is our tether and our Ariadne's thread.

You always stood apart, even then. Everywhere I looked
that day the sea was tame, passive
as a castrate tiger. But you

gone out like a decommissioned lighthouse,
and something wrecked, sinking slowly
amongst the bladderwrack and scum.

I never knew until today
how your blood yearned for the sun;
and you in enduring darkness, lost to the cold.

Visiting Hours

Car's raked by Atlantic westerlies
here where I press faster than I should
as if to outstrip it all; clocking Bodmin's
unclothed spine, knotted with tar and traffic

and the smell cooked into my clothes
rising like a choking fish from a fetid puddle
trapped between rocks, chapping my face
with unbidden pictures, over and over:

where you are a throb of collarbones
stickwrists and sinews, thrashing
your wren-weight wet-eyed to splay against
the sun's blade cutting through glass

pinning you where you dribble your gall
or break the surface with a half-remembered
name, splinters of an ancient gut-lodged hurt
callused and tumoured from decades of weatherbeat

the thin gruel of the present unstomached
along with the past; then the diving back,
the long tunnel into enduring silence,
a century closing over your head

and you huddled into nothing
your eyes turned inward, only into night
– this small patch of March sun that scalds you,
that you can't see; and my hand on yours

lifting the cup to flush the communion
of morphine and flesh, here where we rock together
wordless, here where I can't yet weep, where
I wait for you to be loosed on the downdraught,
the slipstream, at the lip of this cliff.

The air that escapes through the meshes

When poets write of grief
they speak of big things –
oceans, moons, the innumerable shades of blue,
an all-consuming song in a minor key, endlessly replayed.
A Mephistophelian pain.

I think it's not like that.
My grief's a smaller thing, mouse-grey, gnawing the day's edges;
it's a dripping thing, quietly insistent and not beautiful –
no searing soaring cello or jazz sax but
a murmur of rain drizzling a grimy window
a door that sticks and doesn't quite shut even if you kick it
the blackly decaying ribs of that old holed rowing boat
fetched up in the mud
a nobody's vessel, going nowhere, not even downwards.

A poet would speak of the mist that sits
on the farther shore; ignoring the jetsam
(the plastic, the ringpulls and condoms)
he'd write of the tidelines of loss that beach on the
empty swans' nest, not quite out of reach of storm.

But here it is, monochrome: the absence of stubble in the plughole;
the single yogurt in the shopping basket;
the crack in the sole of your favourite shoe
that lets in the wet
and the seeping cold that bit by bit
will claim you.

The grief that takes hold of your lungs and squeezes
is not about what's been lost
but the walls that the air builds between you
the countless ways in which you hold back
scared of being all you might be

scared of falling into love
and keeping on falling
scared of being seen
being seen, being found out naked.

Three For Dharma
for Jack Kerouac

i
On The Road

You died just before I met you.
Not much changes. America, Vietnam.
America, Iraq.

Here we are still sitting,
still praying, those of us who are alive,
like Desolation Angels at the hem of apocalypse

as the earth spins in its dance through space in this
accelerating universe of stars and black holes.
Same diet: hopes, dreams, fears.

Tending the fires. What else is there to do?

ii
Why I live where I do

Seeking freedom
we still live in chains
civilisation gets in the way
fills up the cracks where It
might slip through, sweeps
it all too clean.

What liberate
are these correspondences:
ocean mind, heart speaking to heart,
to be intimate with
sky

cloud
tree.

To travel
beyond the names of things.

iii
That we should be here at all

That we dare to cross these divides –
all that stands between us –
risk shipwreck, falling, drowning
over and over to save these separate selves
from separateness.
                    That we dare.

Tending the fires. Still; what else?

Double Cinquain

Give me
lemons, figs, wild
pomegranates, juicy,
red. Give me your lips, your body,
your bliss.

Give me
the fire from your belly, the taste
of your rage, despair, fear.
Just don't give me
your lies.

Physics Lesson

Optoelectronics: you scribe the tongues
of lithium, niobium – molecules
which rearrange the fabric of us all
as surely, as improbably as love.

I'm picturing tectonics: grinding plates
of continents beneath the heaving oceans
meshing in uneasy shifts beyond the reach
of light, of all our knowing.

This spinning planet's wild arcane interior,
throbbing secret lives, drawn briefly
down to this: this triangle on paper, captive
atoms whirling in their disenfranchised

orbits, knocking on the sides, against each other
in their frenzy to be free   and glyph-less –
these fish-tanks, when what they wanted
                                        was the sea.

Crossing the Desert

Sand cold, wind cold, stars in their
ancient dervish coldness.

Stopped at the edge. Nothing *is* –
not even stars. All capable

of sudden vanishings –
wind sand stars even

people.

Into their own aloneness.
Then it's nothing but dropping

night dropping. Maybe this whole thing
ending. Maybe the horse of your body

hungry. Lame. Listened to this.
Ship of a planet, spinning in –

space. Imagine

this whole thing. Ending. What else but.
Night dropping. Stopped at the edge.

Where silence holds. Listened
a bit. Heard my own blood, then

the distant ocean
singing. Saddled up. Risked

the first step.

Out of Albion

We called it Avalon, isle of apples
honey and eternal youth, this ripe breast
swelling out of the summer country's milky sea;
doorway to the paradise we thought would have no end,
beyond the ripples of all the pairs of opposites,
the tides of blood and bone.
                                                    Flushed with our own
fullness, become accustomed to abundance,
we didn't see how easy it would be, how swift
the betraying journey through veiling mists

and the draining of the waters. And we
left upright, hard and angular, uncoupled
from fins and wings and creeping things,
balanced on legs that would walk us away
from each other, out into dry air
thick with its tumble of dead bees;

and it's only now, beached on stony ground
where our sureness falters and words stumble
after something barely perceived and already
left behind, irretrievable as childhood,
we notice at our feet the flood
of apples, brown glut amongst the burnt-off stubble,
shrivelled, ordinary as yesterday's platitudes,
so soon given over to the wet kiss of decay.

They who can, dance

First frost. October sun skims mist from the river. Goldfinches
charming the air and a congregation of rooks, raucous in black.
Cackling. A place for laughter and a place for tears. Sweetness
and screaming. We go on.

You do not have to be good. You
do not have to be good.

Just listen, pay attention, listen.

By the hedge a fresh kill, small white rabbit-belly exposed,
entrailed. Already the magpie and crow.

In seeking to save your life you will destroy it.

Fox-red bracken slouches against banks; grass bursts tarmac.
Then a place where tarmac stops and the wild world creeps
back. Be badger. Be fox. *Paddle in mud.* Oak leaves, dead now,
crisp underfoot. The old year gone down, not with a bang or a
whimper.

Be
a vessel for the marriage of water and air, fire and earth, light
and dark.

You do not have to be good and do penance.

Here we move our pens, attempt to fix the unfixable. *Then break
the vessel.* Charm the air. They who can, dance.

> Here it is morning
> tide's nadir   Sunlight
> drips from the eaves

Through Rain

'It is / the experience of our world that makes it real / and nothing more.'

Andy Brown

You do not 'do' dogs, or so you declare. We look at each other wryly as the dog, far too big to be a lap-puppy, furtively crouches and half-springs half-wriggles over the arm of your chair to curl on your knee. This touches me absurdly.

> In the room lilies
> shuck off their thick pink
> sexy fragrance

The fire wheezes.

What sustains you when all falls to ashes? The world presents itself in moments – here and here and here – a ripe peach at the point of dropping. The train moves on and we don't see whether the fruit is caught. Everything calls to us for attention. When did we learn to turn away? The lost art of being being simply enough. But moment after moment offered for the plucking. How do we relearn trust? Outside, the rain fumbles at the glass.

The Perfect Tense

Those young faces, smooth, unknown; their perfect limbs and white
                                        whites of eyes –
        the way the world – here at least in England –
has not made holes in them; barely skims their shoulders,
barely pressing. No edges
                        to host shadows.

        I think of my daughter, her face
unnavigated by more than a couple of decades. She is
        a windflower in a dusky wood.
                Impossible to imagine that these collections of atoms
        could have so come together; will one day drift apart.
Impossible to want to imagine.

        Our children: they do not know how smooth their flesh is;
are not aware that the perfect tense is
                here   now   always;

        and how easily it's unmade.

Life, be unbruising; lend them lightness to outweigh
the shadows, lend them
                the perpetual motion of hope.

*

Late afternoon: wind seizes the trees with a madness; the puppy
        skips after fat leaves of hazel, oak, chestnut.
                Clouds piled like grubby pillows in a laundry.

                Later, back home in the field, on a flat stone
a little posse of glow-worms wait for the darkness to step by
        and light them up.

Across the hedges Shetland mares stand with their new young
folded into creases
   among timothy grass and buttercups.
    Moths graze the air.

Now, dusk is slipstreaming calm
        and Venus
pokes through from the other world.

*

'I don't fear death,' said Peter today,
   'only the dying.'

I am now, I realise, one of the initiates who know
   the truth: that death is an inescapable promise;
      a truth that will overtake me, too.

The light through water,
     under the cloud canopy,
is beautiful now, and frail –
   it says it will not last;
and it promises, while it does, that it will loose something
in us
to wander towards the horizon
   and go on wandering.

If you tune everything else out the silence you hear is the white noise
   of the singing spheres: the voice of the universe.

You can never get to its edge
and yet
you could fit millions of universes on the already-crowded head
of that pin, with all those minute-particle-angels.

Come back, Giordano Bruno; they wouldn't burn you
now. Your heresies are old-hat orthodoxy.

The stars are in our belly; the Milky Way
our umbilicus. Is it
a consolation
that the stuff of which we're made is star-stuff too?
That wherever you go you can never totally disappear –
dispersal only: carbon, hydrogen, nitrogen, oxygen.

Tree, rain, coal, glow-worm, horse, gnat, rock.

*

The year
falls away from the zenith
and the rowanberries are rouging up.

The hands tick round.
What will I salvage of this calendar?
The throwing-away process has begun.
Between now and Allhallows falls the equinox:
the opposites poised in perfect creative tension
before the tumble into darkness.

November 1, a new beginning for me
and the Celtic New Year.

Remaking my life.

Maybe.

*

Now, dusk; all the available light –
      yellow, cyan, magenta –
inhaled and re-emitted by cranesbill, loosestrife, muskmallow.

My hand, making these words.

Nightshade

I'm searching for a word, something
like 'curlew' or 'caress';
something to wrap around my tongue
like a twist of lemon dipped
in cream, something
of summer – meadowsweet
rosebay, woodruff –
and its undertow of longing

*

Walking another country.
A haunting, an infiltration

it's about finding, or maybe losing.

Those careful fine-boned hands
the slack-jawed carp beneath –

I'm dissected.

*

– *You*
still take the bends too fast
you said; and you were right.
This need to defy G-force,
the way
        it redefines your face.
The flames at the edges
when you're turning the ton
the pull of faraway constellations
        and night-time daring.

*

How you gobble experience
subsume everything to that need
to consume life whole
                      – it's a tough god
you serve. Put everything
to the test: you can't assay
people, make of them altars
to lost deities. *Try me*

                  *

the way at night in June
it never really darkens
the pelt of warm air
clothing your languid body
how you'd glide easily
from dusk to dawn to dusk
and night a raft of voices
and you not really alone

                  *

but that was before. It's cold
here at night, and colder
with these pictures
of you. Crass
to talk of railway tracks:
lives are never parallel.

                  *

Already the wasps
nibble windfalls, and thistle-
down clots the fields.
Martins twillit in the eaves
all night; flex new primaries

at dawn. Fill the sky. We're
        gearing up to leave.

     *

This provisionality. But how
we push and push
our days, squeeze the last
inch from every moment,
try to lick it clean.

     *

     Today the wind's
in the east.
     This morning, driving back,
I watched lightning
     drag its nails
down the sky, over and over.

     *

Later what scratches holes
on the dark is that gap
between end-on lengths of steel
(these metaphors of journeys)
how it shrinks in the chill
and small things tumble through:
coins, flints, shrew's skull.
The single kiss you unfisted.
(Ah these memories of you.
And how they buckle in the heat.)

Source Nord, 3 a.m.

At three o'clock a little wind gets up
gets up and walks in the garden
At three o'clock a little wind gets up

The creatures of the moon
dance under the moon
dance under the moon

                              everything is permitted
                              everything is blown away

The moon is another country
Her people are the lives
                    we   don't   live

Moon Wood
after Franck André Jamme, *Bois de Lune*

They say that you come here
from time to time, bird on fist
you come and you wait

unlike the bird, quickening
as it does to impatience
to the impulsion of flight

frantic scrabbling to freedom
smell of space permeating leather
and you loosen the jesses

and it's gone

and the forest for one brief moment
sparking to long flame, shimmering

it kills
that's the truth; it kills –
you know it in the boon
laid at your feet, whimpering still
but gone with the long flames

you are blind; your hunting
merely a gathering

you have no memory
of the bird's airborne flutter
nor of the drawn bow of its flight

and all this because
it is within you

it is within you

you are the moon's
long arc cleaving the sky
the light in the hawk's eye
the white cry of the prey

you are the shining
the flame
the scream

you may not yet know where
but all of this
happens
within

Looking For Icarus

Here we eat silence
as heat eats us

the crickets' song
only underlines absence

and every sunflower turning its face
to the sky

reminds us how far we have come
how far we still have
to fall

In Transit

The woodpecker's green laughter
has called us back to ourselves

in the space between the inbreath
and the out, where we vibrate

like the earth at 7.8 Hertz

we sense that beyond and all around us

everything has rearranged itself
molecules subtly remade; and nothing

is quite as it was, even you and I
just a moment ago, before.

Physicke Garden

Jacob can keep his Ladder
with its busy hosts of angels.

This is as close to heaven
as I might wish to be –

this still corner of this spinning world,
your hot tongue on my hot skin,

and outside, somewhere else, a small rain
washing the dust off things.

Like tomorrow

Sometimes in the night I think I hear your footsteps, see you stretch a hand to lead me into your country, your mind which is incandescent with lights like Christmas candles, or still like a deep pool inhabited by golden carp, thoughts which fan the water as delicately as fins, barely rippling; or flick in a shower of neon across to the other shore, leaving me gasping for breath.

Sometimes you arrive like a flamenco dancer; sometimes a small wind swimming through leaves, and as I turn you've already left, and only the trees swaying to show your passage.

Sometimes you are an incantation on the lips of someone else
a vowel not quite uttered
a syllable just caught
a faraway tune.

Sometimes you are a hawk hanging on the wind.

I like it best when I turn from the kitchen where sunlight is stroking the tiles and walk out into the summer morning, grass still wet and the garden shaking off night, and you're there in the extravagance of hibiscus, or under the lime tree; or waiting on the doorstep in the basket of bursting figs, bloom still untouched, like tomorrow.

Memories of Flight (pictures at an exhibition)

1 The Rose Lagoon

Vespers, and a black moon.
But look – here's a softer piece:
for a friend in a faraway country

a rose lagoon, and from its core
a light mist rising, warm and teasing,
a genie in a gilded bottle.

Tell me how swallows navigate home,
over and over – those few grammes
against all the implacable ocean.

11 Evening Light

This painter makes swallows. In a mirror
a nightingale practises migration

and in his turquoise lagoon
flamingoes shimmer with pigment.

He is Icarus. At the point of his brush
everything's possible. In the tip of him.

Later she'll oil his shoulders,
slide her hands lower, release him.

For a moment he'll believe in flying.

111 When Night Comes

Day turns to night, and in the blink
of an eye he knows that

the atoms that bind them together
also hold them apart.

Puigcampana

Waking in the dark, sweating, remembering; shaken
like the shutters in night's rattle.

Later the relief of the peaks, a breeze, astringency
of rosemary and thyme in yellow light; then

there you were again, yesterday, where,
black on aquamarine, the hawk mothing the empty sky
was a shadow at which I clutched,
breathless and dry in this almost-birdless land.

I am not sure if I wanted, then, to fall
into the sky or out of it, whether there was too much air
or not enough. Certainly I wanted to fly
out of myself, be prised apart, eased

out of the creases in which I hide. But you
are not dead; almost I can reel you back in
to safety, as the hawk spools sure
in the great net of sky.

I want to open a passage for you again,
be the resting place that rock is for light.

Against the Ice
Contra el agua, diás de fuego Octavio Paz

There are mornings when you wonder
how anything ever turns out right –

when we're all refugees trudging scorched soil
without hope; without anything;

yet in the face of all odds
snowdrops still break iceblack soil

swollen plums blush in the August sun
despite pollution, genetics and sprays

and there are insects who still know
what pollen to merge with which.

Then there are evenings when out of the stillness
a huge wind rises to stride through the leaves

and sets fat drops of rain glistening
like fairy-lights amongst the mulberries;

And times when the voice of a blackbird
breaks you open

and you go out into everything, your heart
on fire like a sunflower in a landscape

that ripples with song, with something
that cannot be suppressed.

Taking Light

Only in the breaking
　　of something
might we re-member wholeness
　　the measure of it, its encompass.

The earth takes her light in a gulp
　　of 2 kilos per second*
and how we take ours
　　is neat, in unpremeditated doses –

irradiated, for instance, by the faces
　　of all who've loved us.
This is how the fragments
　　hum back into wholeness.

It's unconditional. It continues. It's a fact.
　　This has nothing to do with reason
And does not depend on belief.
　　It continues. This is a fact. Remember light.

with acknowledgement to Charles Wright

Avebury

the journey

taking the serpent path
– Fyfield, Overton (the Sanctuary), West Kennett
                              (with its cargo of dead, long digested
                                    into the sarsen-chambered dust)

where the land thrusts its
                              hummocky wombs at the wide sky
pushes up chalk and flint and bone

                                   while beside me on the A4
                                   the army snakes its tanks
                    to some imagined destiny – an enemy, a bloodshed

                                   another fiction of winning
                                   here where we all lose
                    where all our stories dissolve in the end

                    – this five and a half thousand year old dust

                                   – *forgetting is so long*

– nodding Michaelmas daisies
                    roadside buckets of chrysanths
                              (dusty pinks, pomegranate, rust)

the lapwings are back, rising in clouds
          from the chalkfawn ploughland
                              (tumbled with tides of flint
                                        or raucous with rooks)

rosehips blooding the hedgerows
          and the faintest tracery of green

winter wheat stitching the furrows

we enter the gullet of the Long Barrow
                              as we might enter anaesthetic
                              or first sex, or a Taverner mass

holding our breath
it's always the first time

Silbury's great waiting dome
              pregnant as a question
                              the sky parts like water around her

we remember this land

              its pulse throbs in our blood

tracking these pairs of stones
one and a half miles of serpent belly

– older than Christ, than the Buddha

past the 'Sarsen Pet-Grooming Parlour'
              – string of racehorses on the horizon, watercolour sky
                      caterpillars of trees crawling up hillsides

crop circles baled, safe-stacked in neat pyramids
(we put away our mysteries like dissidents)

and nearing now the two solitary long stones
                              – outriders, waymarkers, promises

and early this October morning
                              (the car park full)

Enter the Temple

– ice cream vans, motors snorting grey into white chill
                                        we all want answers
                        but an ice cream might offer relief

– these stones, rocked in their long sleep

ash trees whispering, this shared dream
                                – dog walkers, bright anoraks,
a cat
            someone shooting

and the robins
a single seagull exiled on the wind, a tourist

a scatter of beech leaves, bright on the tarmac like coins
offerings to the winter gods

we come for answers, questions, to pray, to remember, to forget

                                        (– *loving is so short*)

the road bisects our circle
                    divides us each from the other
                            halved
            (sun and moon in their separate stone-spun orbits)

– the village hall offers bingo, line-dancing
and on the road a mess of fox
deflecting tyres, clutching my breath –

the threshold

the lives under our feet
                   these sheep-tracks, chalk bones poking
                     – east wind, the traffic hum

– these pitted surfaces, a freckling of holes
            a milky way on sarsen

I feel your stone cheek, rest my face
            – your moss-lined tiny craters
                      stone acne, age-pocks

and the dribble of lichen down
            your northern face

(these sad concrete facsimiles – markers –
'what might have been, we think')

imagine ploughing these up – 5000 years –
this long stone night – gone between one turn
of the giant feathered fetlocks and the next;
buried, smashed, recycled into a new age of the secular;

imagine not knowing.

                    'Demolished by Tom Robinson 1700
                          ...taken away 1718
                          ...taken away 1719
                          ...taken away 1720

                                                    ...broke 1722
                                        ...broke off to the stumps'

Imagine not knowing.
Tom Robinson what have you done
(and you weren't alone) –
fear, need, ignorance, greed –
I stand where you stood
and I can't weep

– the inner ring all extracted or amputated, here where the earth
                                                                aches
                              dreams the ghosts of stones

                        (another century sliding downhill)

you're tilting now, falling back into
                    your own time, your own dream
                              into the earth's pull

a cathedral of silence, a web, this network we inhabit –
            these filaments, no less tangible for being invisible
                        holding us, Indra's net, a cradle

                        – pass through, feel the texture of silence
                          the dancing circle, mandala, songlines

                                    laced we are each to each

suddenly now I want to cry, to lie on my back
                    here in this womb, this egg, on this edge
to howl at the gunmetal sky

in this dream I hold you, whisper

the open ditch, across which
                    she must have crawled, bleeding –
                              so many deaths

                         – into the long night

the long passionless dreaming stone night

but in the heart of the egg a pulse

                    all born of sea, its tides

                    et in Arcadia ego

– a late daisy, a Mars bar wrapper, the trees turning
                              – spice, copper, plum

still, under the traffic
               our doubts our fears our hopes
                         the tides of us

– thinking you might be here suddenly
                    – just around the next corner in time

materialising like summer, unbidden
                    the thought's enough

               in another country we're standing side-by-side

                    – the lichen here thick like emulsion

         – a tasteless eau-de-nil
     but dusted with a ransom of gold

– and we're walking the serpent sarsen way
         hoping to step out of ourselves

         out of these binding skins
         (time a construct, a
         palimpsest,

         a fiction sketched on air)

weaving and looping

walking on chalk bones –
eroded here, the grass damp, dunged

(the sheep dreadlocked, thick pile fleece
gentle-faced, curious, clicking their heads
around in second-hand jerks, yellow-eyed, sniffing the wind)

presence

then this omphalos, this womb

         this heartbeat

anchor, lynchpin, *axis mundi*

     in and out of time

making the circle, the figure of eight
       to infinity, double helix, möbius

and the end was the beginning

where all our fictions meet

the heart's temple, sanctuary
here
this place we never leave

it's <u>this</u> the poem; all our words inept

the return

– voices, a football, kids throwing themselves
rolypoly down damp ditch slopes and ramparts
October
– lovers families photos anoraks the traffic's hum
(like a landbound sea)

– grey light, east wind

(smell of toast, coffee, someone roasting chestnuts
the manor, tearooms, pond holding sky)

and you become newly alone, become

almost lost, who nearly

didn't come back from
the serpent's egg

the serpent's open mouth

this long colon of darkness

taking the serpent path

beyond sea

beyond sky

beyond love

beyond death

here

where all

our stories meet

in the beginning

is the end

Meditation

Thunder speaking in tongues
and the buzzard's high mew

the voice of the bell

and then only silence
dropping
like
petals

Notes

In the opening sequence of prose poems, *West,* the phrase 'dying fall' of course comes from T S Eliot; I have also paraphrased his famous 'Till human voices wake us, and we drown'. The two 'St Ives' pieces in this sequence contain references to the Sea of Clear Glass. These passages are adapted from the C12th Celtic text *The Book of the Dun Cow,* translated by Dr Whitley Stokes in C19th, and appearing in *Myths and Legends of the Celtic Race,* by T W Rolleston (Constable 1985).

The reference to the black and white sails in 'St Ives' is from the legend of Tristan and Iseult. In the legend Tristan's living or dying hangs on the colour of the sails on the boat approaching the castle from across the sea to where he lies wounded in Brittany. If white, it means that his true love, the first Iseult and the only person who can heal him, is on her way. His wife, the second Iseult, lies to him about the colour of the sails; she says they are black. Consequently he turns to the wall and dies, just minutes before the fair first Iseult walks in.

The Perfect Tense: Giordano Bruno was a mediaeval 'heretic' and alchemist burnt at the stake for many reasons, one of which was that he challenged the orthodoxy of the time by suggesting that, in fact, the earth rotates around the sun, not vice versa.

Roselle Angwin

Indigo Dreams Publishing
24 Forest Houses
Halwill
Beaworthy
Devon
EX21 5UU
United Kingdom
www.indigodreams.co.uk